FOREWORD

Your search for the ideal home-based business may be over. The home retail bait business is great for retirees, homemakers, even kids! The business makes a great family project that everyone can be involved in. If you have a love of the outdoors, particularly fishing, you can turn that experience into an extra asset with a retail bait shop. If you enjoy visiting with people, you'll fit right in with storytelling fishermen! With this guide in your hands, you have a complete directory of information: Names, addresses, telephone numbers and web sites. What to get, where to get it and why. "Trade secrets" and tips to increase your chances for success. With decades of experience in the bait business, I have learned plenty of lessons. This guide also includes some things you should avoid. Had it been available when I started, this guide would have saved me from some mistakes! The benefit of my experience is now yours. So, let's give it a shot!

This could be the business for you.

© Copyright 2018

Beaumont Books

10 9 8 7 6

ISBN 978-1985361799

The Home Bait Shop – *Steps to Success*

LOCATION, LOCATION, LOCATION!

As in real estate, the location of your bait shop is very important. Although it is not necessary to be located adjacent to prime fishing water, there must be at least some available fishing within a few miles of your shop. Fishermen will travel to get good bait... available when they want it. However, if you are limited to your current location, examine fishing areas available within a ten to twenty mile radius. Your aim will be a steady customer base (perhaps seasonal), within your market area. If the potential isn't there, you should examine other options.

Competition is something to consider. Well-established bait shops are tough to compete with. If an established bait shop exists within a few miles of your proposed location, you may wish to reconsider. Splitting available business does little favor for either party, and makes a profitable operation that much less likely to achieve. This is not to say that every established bait retailer is invulnerable, just be sure you have realistic expectations of available revenue and potential profits.

The location of your shop on your property is quite important. All factors being equal, your first choice should be a basement or below grade area. The cooler temperatures involved will make keeping the bait much easier. A garage or outbuilding would be good second and third choices.

The Home Bait Shop – *Steps to Success*

You should keep the following factors in mind when locating your shop. We'll discuss them in order.

1. Availability of water.
2. Accessibility for customers (and you).
3. Room (about 300 square feet makes a nice start).
4. Security and safety.
5. Electricity.

---

1. Water is a necessity if you intend to sell live minnows. (For the purposes of our discussion I will refer to live baitfish as simply "minnows", without incorporating regional names for the product.) As will be discussed in greater detail in a later chapter, the technical requirements are quite simple for the use of well or spring water. Not only must the supply of water be considered, we also must consider its disposal. Storm sewers or similar means of disposal for 'used' water will be discussed in a later chapter.

---

2. Your shop needs to be accessible...for both customers and you. You don't want customers to have to walk through your home to reach your shop. By the same token, you don't want to have to go outside every time a customer arrives (unless, of course, your shop is located

The Home Bait Shop – *Steps to Success*

separate from your house). A dedicated outside entrance to your shop is ideal. Sometimes outside access to your basement is available. If so, consider placement of the shop area close to this access. <u>Plan your own steps now, so that your movement will be efficient.</u>

Parking is a concern. Your driveway will probably serve as parking at the start of your business. Later, if growth warrants, more parking may be required. (What a great thought!) Consider your neighbors (if you have some) and how parking may affect their property. It pays to be thoughtful and respectful of others...literally. Staying on good terms with neighbors will help with your word of mouth advertising.

---

3. Square footage can be a difficult question. My guideline of approximately 300 square feet makes for a nice-sized shop...enough room to accommodate minnow tank(s), displays, and customers! Again, growth is something to keep in mind. Partition separation of the retail area from unused space in your basement or garage (or other shop location) is essential. This also will allow for easy removal/relocation of partitions if you wish to expand. Another benefit of partitions is to disconnect your shop area from your personal family storage area. Let's face it; we all accumulate "stuff." In the interest of keeping your shop area clean and orderly, *which is essential*, it's much easier if you have a separate place for your other belongings. Keeping your shop clean, well-lit

The Home Bait Shop – *Steps to Success*

and orderly is much easier to do if there's less of it. Also, starting small keeps your costs manageable.

---

4. Security is no small matter. The ability to lock your shop when you are away is very important. It's also important that you are aware when customers arrive. A simple electric-eye type bell or buzzer can alert you to customers. Door-mounted switches can also announce an arrival. This also serves the practical purpose of serving the customer quickly.

Safety of customers is serious business. Safe, clean, well-lighted access to your shop prevents accidents. Take special notice of stairways. I cannot place enough emphasis on prevention...keep it safe. Lighting is important enough to mention again. Your shop area (particularly stairways) should be bright and easy to navigate.

Insurance is a special concern. A standard homeowner policy may not be enough. I'll have more on this subject.

---

5. Electricity is essential in a retail operation. As mentioned above, adequate lighting provides safety as well as a better selling environment. Typical household electrical service is normally adequate for a retail bait shop. The addition of commercial grade lighting and perhaps a small refrigerator or two does not usually place

The Home Bait Shop – *Steps to Success*

an excessive burden on your electrical system. Older systems, or new installations in an outbuilding, will probably require professional help. If in doubt, contact a qualified electrician for an opinion.

Once you've settled on the location for your shop, we're ready to move on.

The Home Bait Shop – *Steps to Success*

HOW TO START

I. Licenses and Permits. A sales tax permit will be required. Contact your state revenue office to inquire about procedures. Usually, all that's required is a simple form stating essential information. In most states, bait is taxable. You will be collecting sales tax on your bait sales, and then forwarding the collected tax to your state, usually monthly or quarterly, depending upon the volume of sales. Often the entire process from applying for a license to submitting tax collected can be done via the Internet. In addition, some states require a license to sell live bait. There is usually a small fee, as this license is a form of tax. Contact your state fish and wildlife division to see if such a license is required. Again, using the Internet for contact will save you time.

Some communities license businesses. As local requirements vary widely, it is best to check with local authorities to determine if a special license will be required to operate.

Liability insurance should be a necessity. Slips and falls are a real possibility in a retail environment. Your insurance agent can be a great source of information on what policy will protect you in the event of injury on your property. Don't assume that a "homeowner" policy will cover this type of use. Often such policies specifically disclaim any type of commercial activity. Again, check with your agent for information unique to your situation.

The Home Bait Shop – *Steps to Success*

Although incorporating your business may be advisable, it is easier (and cheaper) to simply operate your business as a proprietorship during the early stages of the business. A proprietorship treats income and expenses from your business as simply an extension of your personal finances. Although the benefits of incorporation are many, it often makes sense to see if your business is viable before spending large sums of money on its initial structure. If your plan includes renting a facility (which defeats many of the advantages outlined in this guide), you should certainly retain the services of a knowledgeable accountant and attorney to advise you. This guide is not intended as a substitute for sound accounting and legal representation.

II. Zoning. This is one area that may give you problems. Depending upon the zoning of your property, and the degree of enforcement, you may not be able to open a commercial enterprise on your property. Although your project is most likely an "incidental use" to the property (that is, not the primary use of the premises...living quarters being the primary use), some zoning simply will not allow commercial use on residential property.

Zoning regulations can be as varied as the communities they are in. It's best to check with a local zoning official to determine. Sometimes all that's required is a permit to conduct the activity you anticipate. Again, check with a local authority. To ignore zoning laws may result in fines and/or having to close your business after you've opened.

The Home Bait Shop – *Steps to Success*

Take the right road and save yourself problems and expense later on.

III. Signage. Your business will need at least one sign to let potential customers know where you are. As discussed in the section on zoning, local regulations often cover sign size and placement. Sometimes a permit (yes, yet another tax) is required to erect a sign on your property. Checking with local authorities first can prevent problems later. **The sign should not be complex.** We're selling a simple product. A neat sign with the words "LIVE BAIT" in bold, clean letters, an arrow pointing to your shop and, perhaps, a sharp outline of a fish is all that is needed. Avoid the temptation to become elaborate with the sign. A cluttered sign gains nothing. Your name isn't even necessary, save that for your business cards.

Your local phone book will have listings under "Signs" or "Sign Painters" that will point you in the right direction. New varieties of plastic signs with vinyl cutout lettering are now available. Neat, quick and sturdy, these new plastic creations can get you going quickly and with minimal expense. Your local sign painter or awards shop can easily show you some options.

The Home Bait Shop – *Steps to Success*

Lighting of the sign, particularly during early morning hours, is key. If zoning permits lighting of signs, by all means do. Consider efficient LEDs. A simple timer or photocell can operate the lights on your sign with no intervention from you. A lighted sign is a 24-hour-a-day salesman for your business, and you can't beat the price!

IV. Hours of Operation Fishing is, mostly, an early-morning activity. As such, your bait shop would do well to take advantage of the necessary hours. When I first started, my bait shop hours were from 4:30 in the morning until 8 at night. As the years went by, I became slightly less ambitious! 7-days-a-week is almost a necessity. It pays to note that many discount stores open too late in the morning to be of interest to serious anglers. <u>You gain a big advantage by opening early.</u>

Hours of operation calls for a degree of commitment. If your shop is a family project, it makes it easier to spread out the necessary time. My shop hours eventually settled at 5 A.M. to 5 P.M., every day. Customers learn to expect (and depend!) on your hours, so **consistency is important**.

There are many opinions about having a 'day off'. Although time to yourself is nice, one of the main advantages of The Home Bait Shop is that you are often available anyway, and can thereby offer attractive hours to your customers. It pays to think of the angler who just drove an hour out of his way to buy bait from you. It would be unfortunate to have a potential good regular customer find that you are closed.

The Home Bait Shop – *Steps to Success*

I know some dealers who have different hours for each day of the week. While you may be able to keep track of it, your customers are not that focused on it. Consider keeping your hours the same each day of the week. Closing early (or staying open late) one or two days a week isn't harmful, but you should keep your hours as easy to remember as possible. (It also takes less space on your business cards!)

Bait vending machines have been popular in recent years. Roughly the size of a refrigerator, these units vend packages of bait much like a soda machine. A vending machine gives you the ability to offer 24 hour service.

Check out a fantastic lineup of machines at www.livebaitvending.com or call Gary at 610-942-2185. You may find that a vending machine can serve most of your business without actually opening (or even having) your shop. These machines have become very popular with existing bait shop owners wishing to increase revenue without expanding hours or adding more employees.

Another option to consider is using multiple machines throughout a region to provide bait service. Many operators have been successful at putting routes together with several machines thus servicing customers in a larger area. This also helps increase dealer buying power, getting a better price for inventory.

The Home Bait Shop – *Steps to Success*

Although the machines are somewhat costly, financing is available. You may be surprised at how easily you can put together a business in your area by simply putting out a few vending machines for bait. The concept isn't new, and it is a proven business plan that has made many operators quite successful.

One quick note on operating multiple machines: It is advisable to stick with one manufacturer and model. That makes it less costly to stock a small supply of replacement parts, and also makes it easier to work on the machines as you will be familiar with their quirks.

The Home Bait Shop – *Steps to Success*

TYPES OF BAIT TO SELL

Fishing baits in different regions of the country can vary widely. I'll attempt to outline the most basic and popular baits that work well nearly anywhere. If you are not fairly experienced at fishing, the guidance of competent bait wholesalers (don't worry, I'll provide some contacts) is essential in tailoring your offerings to your geography. A basic knowledge of fishing bait is helpful, but not completely necessary. That said, it will be much easier to understand the different types of bait available if you already have a grasp of fishing.

Nightcrawlers (also known as dew worms, fish worms or other variations) will, most likely, provide the backbone of your business. You can buy Nightcrawlers from

The Home Bait Shop – *Steps to Success*

wholesalers either in bulk or pre-cupped in ready to sell containers. No additional counting or packing is required for pre-cupped bait. When buying your Nightcrawlers, insist on the best size available. Nightcrawlers are sold commercially based on weight. 6 or 7 pound worms are common; 10 pound worms are outstanding (and tend to be costly). Canadian Nightcrawlers packaged under the **Jumbo®** brand name I have found to be consistently high quality and plump. Like anything else, you pay more for higher quality, but your customers will notice the difference. Wholesale prices for Nightcrawlers start at about $60.00 per thousand (when purchased in bulk), but can vary widely.

Of course, the least costly way is to collect Nightcrawlers yourself. Any warm, damp evening (following rain is best) will allow Nightcrawlers to appear in areas they inhabit. Freshly-tilled farmland, large lawn or golf course fairways will almost always have a decent population of the bigger worms. With a little practice, collecting them will be a profitable way to spend a few hours per evening when the weather is right.

For those familiar with Nightcrawler harvesting, here are a few quick tips to increase your harvest: Use a red colored flashlight. Red light is less noticeable to the worms. A miner-type lamp (with headband) allows you to use both hands. Sawdust can be used to keep your fingers dry. Wear soft shoes, such as sneakers, or go barefoot! It's much quieter to the vibration-sensitive worms and will increase your harvest. Avoid areas (such

The Home Bait Shop – *Steps to Success*

as golf course greens) that have been chemically treated. The bigger worms tend to avoid those areas as well. With wholesale prices well over five cents per worm, gathering your own worms can be quickly profitable.

Supply and demand has a great influence on the price of Nightcrawlers. I can recall paying well over $120.00 per thousand one particularly dry summer, but when a holiday weekend is coming (and you cannot afford to be without worms) it can be well worth it.

Redworms (also known as red wigglers, Trout Worms, Dug Worms) are also popular. This bait, although smaller than Nightcrawlers, is particularly popular during spring trout seasons. As with Nightcrawlers, supply and demand dictate price. Expect prices in the range of $50.00 per thousand as a starting point. However...all worms are not the same.

I should point out that this bait has been replaced, so to say, in recent years by hybrid Redworms imported from Belgium. In my opinion, these Belgian 'manure worms' are inferior in every respect to worms that are harvested from river banks throughout North America.

Belgian worms have also drawn the attention of some environmentalists, as the worms are not native to North America. When released into the wild, the Belgian worms can quickly overtake native worms, and can lead to decimation of topsoil layers. While I don't entirely agree

The Home Bait Shop – *Steps to Success*

with that assessment, it is a concern to quite a few people. No matter how one feels about it, true dug worms are native, and are not a threat to the native worm population in North America.

One company that has rejected the Belgian manure worms and still provides genuine "Dug Worms" is Jumbo Bait Company. www.jumbobait.com Jumbo Bait sells Dug Worms under the trademarked name, "Duggers." Available packaged in sturdy, retail-ready containers of 18 worms, Jumbo Duggers are favored by seasoned anglers, and do not present the alleged environmental concerns that are a hallmark of the Belgian variety.

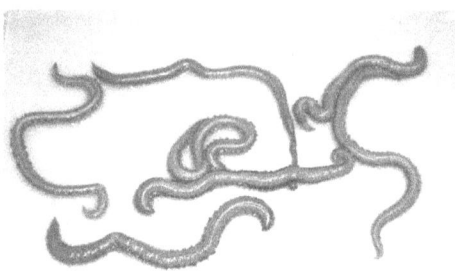

Salt water anglers are fond of **Bloodworms**. Dug from tidal flats in Maine, bloodworms have been popular shore bait for decades. Shipped via overnight freight direct from Maine, bloodworms are somewhat costly, but extremely effective. Bloodworms are even more perishable than most live bait, so you should keep your inventory limited to what you can sell in a few days.

The Home Bait Shop – *Steps to Success*

Maine Bait of Millbridge, Maine has been producing and shipping bloodworms since 1950. Contact them at 207-956-0708, or on the web at www.mainebait.com

---

Mealworms (sold generically as Giant Mealworms, Mighty Mealys and meal bugs) are a premier trout and pan fish bait. Supply and demand tends to have little effect on prices for this bait.

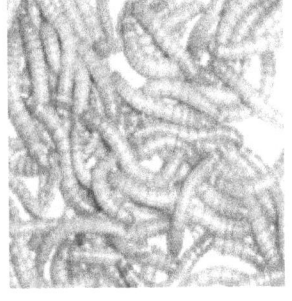

Availability can be an issue in the peak demand of the spring. Expect prices in the $19.00 per thousand-. Shipping is additional, as usual. Often Mealworms can be found packed in retail containers, ready to sell. www.jumbomealworms.com is a dependable supplier.

Waxworms are sometimes in tight supply. Again, a premier trout and pan fish bait. Expect prices of $25.00 per thousand. Shipment via Priority Mail or overnight services from **King's Wholesale Bait**, Post Office Box 183, Liberty, Indiana 47353 765-458-6968 .

The Home Bait Shop – *Steps to Success*

Crickets have long been popular bait. Raised on farms in the Southern United States, crickets have seen resurgence as pet food. Most pet shops carry crickets for customers feeding their lizards, frogs, turtles or any number of other small pets. This is a good way to get some off season business into your shop as these small pets require food all year around, not just during prime fishing months. Setting your shop up as a dependable source for crickets will gain you a loyal clientele who may also buy other items (such as mealworms) all year long.

Crickets are best held at slightly warmer than room temperature. Often a 20 gallon aquarium makes a good cricket box that is easy to keep clean and displays the crickets for better sale. Water and food should be provided, and your wholesaler will be able to provide guidance for best results.

Hatley's Cricket Ranch is a premium producer of live crickets. Shipping via overnight express, Hatley's delivers quality product direct to your door. Contact them at 1-(662) 895-4180, or 7642 Highway 178, Olive Branch, MS 38654.

Minnows (also known regionally as golden shiners, fatheads, rosy reds, redfins, silver shiners, killies and herring) make up the bulk of the live fishbait category. Usually sold by the pound, prices tend to remain steady regardless of supply. The nation's most popular minnow

The Home Bait Shop – *Steps to Success*

type, the **Arkansas Golden Shiner**, is raised commercially at hatcheries in the south central United States. Raised specifically for use as fishing bait, the Arkansas Golden Shiner is particularly hardy and well adapted for holding and transporting. Depending upon your location in relation to the source for these minnows, you can expect prices to range from $6.00 to $15.00 per pound. Size of the bait also affects prices. This bait is graded by size based on the number of pounds required to have 1,000 fish. Thus, a #12 Golden Shiner would require 12 pounds per 1000 fish. A #20 would require 20 pounds, and so forth. Sizes can vary widely…from 3 pounds per 1,000 for the smallest size to over 50 pounds per 1,000 for the largest. Grading of the minnows is accomplished by literally straining the fish through a grader basket, with aluminum bars accurately spaced at specific distances to yield specific sized fish. Grader spacing is indicated in 64^{ths} of an inch, with 19, 24, 27, and 32 being common.

Anderson Minnow Farms in Lonoke, Arkansas is the world's largest producer of Arkansas Golden Shiners. With distributors throughout the United States, Anderson's also has a program to ship their minnows in small quantities direct to dealers via Federal Express.

Find more details at Anderson's web site: www.andersonminnows.com With fast overnight shipping, there isn't any way to get fresher bait.

Anderson's also offers premium bait known as the **Black Salty.** Prized for coastal fishing, the tough and durable

The Home Bait Shop – *Steps to Success*

Black Salty minnow also excels in inland waters for stripers. www.blacksalty.com

---

Crayfish (also known as crawdads, crabs and mini-lobsters) are an excellent catfish and bass bait. Raised commercially throughout the United States, crayfish have always been popular near large cities in the northeast. Available through many minnow wholesalers, expect prices to start at $70.00 per 1,000.

Leeches do well in many parts of the country. Similar to Nightcrawlers in appearance, leeches offer exceptional strength and durability. Leeches are popular in areas with large bream populations. Sunfish and similar species cannot dislodge a leech from the hook with the same ease as Nightcrawlers. This makes leeches popular in you wish to avoid 'nuisance' fish and concentrate on trophy specimens. Expect prices in the range of $50.00 per 1,000. Although sometimes hard to find, leeches are often available through local minnow wholesalers.

Care instructions for all of the above products can best be obtained from the producer or wholesaler. Experience in handling leads to greater success, but basic instruction is always provided by the best wholesale dealers. They want you to be successful, mainly because you will sell more bait!

The Home Bait Shop – _Steps to Success_

As with any perishable commodity, expect losses. Experience will serve to keep your losses at a minimum, but perfection is next to impossible. In fact, your pricing strategy should include allowances for product death loss. There is no way around it, so be prepared. As your depth of experience grows, you will be able to lessen your death loss expense. Unfortunately, you must learn by doing.

Many other regional baits are available that may do well in your area. Various frozen baits such as chicken livers or cut shad could be big sellers, turning fine profits. If you fish, you may very well have a grip on specifics for your region. If not, a good wholesaler can guide your selection, and stock your shop for success.

The baits listed here represent the most popular and available baits on a nationwide basis. Based on your location, some of these may be entirely unsuitable for your operation. Again, proper guidance is essential. Prices listed are averages. As with most items, savings can be had by purchasing in quantity. Also, timing your purchases to avoid periods of shortages (and peak prices) can be worth the trouble, once you master the art of keeping the bait alive. Off-peak buying can result in substantial savings, and is worth the effort.

Trial and error leads to experience. Experience leads to savings and ultimate success.

The Home Bait Shop – *Steps to Success*

The Home Bait Shop – *Steps to Success*

EQUIPMENT AND START-UP

For the storage of Nightcrawlers, Redworms, mealworms and waxworms, a good, used refrigerator is all you need. Often used appliance stores (or recycling yards) offer usable refrigerators for $25.00 to $100.00. This unit will be the core of your business. As your business grows, you can easily add more capacity simply by picking up another used unit. Resist the temptation to purchase new for this use. A workable unit does not have to be pretty. Add a coat of paint if you must, but save the extra expense of buying new. Spend more money on advertising if you have extra cash.

Although waxworms (for example) don't require refrigeration, the other baits do well at 35 to 45 degrees. Indeed, temperatures above 65 put stress on the bait and will likely increase your losses.

Minnows are best held in cool water, 45 to 55 degrees. Certain types of specialized baits require specific temperatures...ask your wholesaler. In general, old cast-iron or fiberglass bathtubs often make excellent starter minnow tanks (I even know some dealers that have been using an old bathtub for minnows for decades.) Easily positioned at waist level in your shop (no bending over!), a bathtub can be a convenient center for your water-based baits. As your business grows, it is easy to add another couple of tubs to expand your capacity.

The Home Bait Shop – *Steps to Success*

If old bathtubs are in short supply, another good option is new black plastic stock tanks from **Rubbermaid**. These tanks are used to water farm animals, and are extremely durable and are priced reasonably. Available at Agway, Tractor Supply or similar farm supply outlets, the minimum size you should consider is 125 gallons…250 gallons is even better.

One option for minnow tanks consists of a self-contained, refrigerated tank with integrated filter and aeration. **Living Stream** units are attractive and do an excellent job. Tank sizes are from 75 to 400 gallons. Check out their web site at: www.frigidunits.com or call Frigid Units, Inc. at 419-478-4000.

The ultimate bait tank would be constructed of concrete block (or poured concrete) resting on a poured concrete slab or floor. This setup allows the coolness of the slab to help keep the water temperature down. The inside of the tank should be coated with any of the popular pond coating materials such as Pond Armor. This will waterproof the tank and provide a smooth, hard surface to facilitate cleaning. Multiple coats may be needed, depending upon the porosity of the tank walls. Your aim should be to completely fill as many pores as possible, thereby making the finished surface even. Don't aim for perfection, but certainly try to make the tank walls free of sharp edges and deep holes. You can purchase Pond Armor direct from the company website at: www.pondarmor.com

The Home Bait Shop – *Steps to Success*

Concrete block or poured concrete tanks offer the ultimate in durability and performance. Such tanks are certainly a commitment, so take your time in planning. You will be satisfied with the result.

I don't recommend this type of tank initially because of its cost and permanence. Odds are you will wish to make changes in your shop layout as your business develops. It's always nice to be able to do things over without great expense or trouble. If your business is successful, you will be able to design the perfect layout to set in stone (literally) at a later time.

The Home Bait Shop – *Steps to Success*

If your shop is in a basement (as previously discussed), temperature control for the water will be less of a concern. The cooler environment of a basement will aid your goal of keeping the water cool. Systems are available (at substantial cost) for cooling the water with a refrigeration unit (see the above-mentioned **Living Stream** units). If your shop is in an outside shed, consider a small room air conditioner to keep the temperature cool during periods of extreme heat. The investment will pay off with lower losses. There is also the comfort factor to consider…for yourself as well as your customers.

Supply water plumbing should be of the plastic variety. The common household method, copper, should be avoided. Copper pipes actually slowly dissolve, releasing copper into the water within the pipes. Copper is toxic to minnows. Although chemicals are available to lessen the effect of copper in your water, it is best avoided as a piping method. The less you have to spend on chemicals for water treatment means more cash left over as profit.

If you have a well, you are among the fortunate of those selling bait. If you will be using city or municipal water, a chemical such as **Better Bait** will be necessary to remove the chlorine and fluoride normally added to public water systems. www.sure-life.com Better Bait imparts a blue tint to the water. This blue color can be something of an advertising value to the fisherman. The "blue water" from the bait shop seems to add confidence that the bait is well cared for, and the chemicals do aid in keeping the bait in better shape in the customer's bucket.

The Home Bait Shop – *Steps to Success*

Perception counts a lot in this business. Just as your customers can be reassured by the color of your water, they can also be uncertain as to the quality of your bait if you have dead minnows in with the live ones. Keep casualties cleared out at all times. You customers want to see live bait, not dead bait. This also plays in to the concept of keeping things neat and clean.

The same is also true about segregation of sizes. Keeping sizes and types of bait easy to distinguish takes some planning, but makes the buying experience that much easier for your customer. An orderly progression of sizes (or types) of bait makes for a better buying experience.

AERATION

Aeration of the tank water is a necessity. A specialized unit known as a **Mino-Saver** works great for water aeration. You can buy Mino-Saver units direct at www.mino-saver.com. A Mino-Saver is an electrically operated unit, approximately 15" high. The bottom half, with paddle and screen, is immersed into the tank water up to an indicated mark. The upper portion, containing a 1/20 horsepower motor, remains above water and dry. The action of the spinning paddle causes circulation and aeration of the tank water. In smaller tanks, such as a bathtub, the Mino-Saver should be placed at the shallow end of the tank (away from the drain and overflow). This will allow the minnows to escape the turbulence created by the aerator, if they desire. This placement will also tend to force fish waste products toward the overflow and drain.

The Home Bait Shop – *Steps to Success*

It is important to retain and use the three-prong plug on the Mino-Saver. This provides a margin of safety for both the bait and operator (you)!

There are many new systems employing air pumps and stones for aerating bait tanks. In my experience, nothing matches the dependability and performance of the Mino-Saver units. In addition, most air pumps impart some amount of heat to the water...a situation we try to avoid. The Mino-Saver units have their power unit (motor) located out of the water. Heat from the motor is rejected into the air, not the water. Again, another plus for keeping water temperature down.

Mino-Saver units are somewhat noisy, but this can also be a benefit. The noise produced by the Mino-Saver unit is a reminder that minnow life support is operating and all is well. Indeed, you will come to notice the sound (or lack thereof) and be reassured by it.

In my own shop, the sound of the aerators in the basement has become common. A power failure is immediately noticeable by me, day or night, due to the sudden end of the familiar Mino-Saver noise. In the unlikely event that the Mino-Saver unit should fail, the lack of noise would allow you to take immediate steps to provide for the bait. Indeed, it is often advisable to have a spare Mino-Saver unit on hand for just such situations.

Additionally, don't discount the advertising value of the sound and action of a Mino-Saver unit. When the

The Home Bait Shop – *Steps to Success*

customer enters your shop, the distinctive sound of water aeration makes a visit to your shop more of an event for the customer. Subtle conditions make a memorable experience. You want your customer to remember your shop, and think of you whenever they think of live bait.

> On edit: The company manufacturing Mino-Saver units has struggled lately. Another manufacturer offering similar units is Boatcycle. www.boatcycle.com Boatcycle's units have duplicated the Mino-Saver design and work just as well.

Your tank should be drained and cleaned (no soap or detergents are necessary, just a basic wipe-down and rinse) between loads of minnows. Draining is much easier if your tank can be equipped with piping from the overflow/drain to a basement sump or outside drain. If you have a dry well or other convenient place to dispose of your 'used' water, by all means take advantage of it. Having standing water outside should be avoided, unless of course you are draining into an existing pond. Draining into a septic system is also a poor choice, as the used minnow water often contains insufficient waste material for proper digestion in a septic system.

Ease of cleaning your tank(s) means you will clean more often, which will be good for your product. Like anything else, doing something often enough makes you aware of what is easy and what is not. Experience will be your guide.

The Home Bait Shop – *Steps to Success*

Be sure to consider wintertime operation. No matter if you plan on being open in the winter or not, you still must consider if your piping will freeze Think about both supply piping and drains. Heat tape may be used if you anticipate freezing. Your local hardware store can provide guidance.

It is worth noting that if you are considering heating your shop in the winter months, you need not keep it at room temperature (71 degrees is considered typical household room temperature). In fact, your bait will benefit by keeping the temperature on the cool side.

Consider nothing higher than 55 degrees. Plenty warm enough to take off the chill, but not so warm as to add

excessive heating cost to eat into the profits of your enterprise.

For holding different sizes of minnows in a single tank, wooden boxes are easy to build with four sides and plastic mesh on the bottom. This box will float in the larger tank allowing separation by size or type of bait. Home improvement stores such as Home Depot or Lowes now carry plastic material in plank form. Consider using plastic rather than wood for

The Home Bait Shop – *Steps to Success*

greater durability in this application. The white plastic boards I have seen also look sharp, keeping your shop looking clean and modern.

You will need some type of net to catch the bait and count them out into your customers' buckets. Two nets are best...one to corral a quantity of minnows, and a second (smaller) net to actually count out the bait. The floating boxes mentioned above makes this process easier, keeping a quantity available for easy counting.

Dipping the bait bucket into your tank water should be avoided. You never know what a customer has used his bucket for in the past, and the contamination could enter the water in your tank, causing loss. To eliminate this chance, use a plastic milk bottle with the top cut off. You can scoop water from your tank and pour it into the bucket...without risking the water in your holding tank. This also gives a little last minute aeration to the bucket water. Be sure to check inside the bucket before adding water. You never know what you might find in there.

The Home Bait Shop – *Steps to Success*

Tip: I've found it best to never supply free containers for minnows. This gives you to opportunity to sell bait buckets to customers without a bucket of their own. A small selection of buckets can be added to your shop without excessive investment. You should notice a fair profit margin on your sales of bait buckets, and each bucket should ALWAYS have a sticker with your name and phone number on it for advertising purposes. I'll have more on this subject as it is quite important.

Challenge Plastic Products is a leading manufacturer of bait buckets. Challenge Plastics has a wide selection and has distributors nationwide.

Consider having a selection of three or four different sizes of buckets. This gives a good choice for all budgets. You can buy buckets direct at www.fishingbuckets.com

ADD-ON SALE ALERT!!!

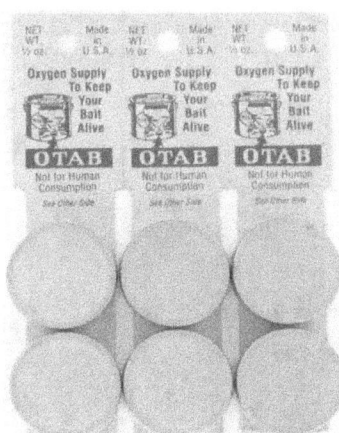

Another important item to offer your minnow customers is a small metal-wrapped tablet that provides oxygen to the water in the bucket. **OTABS** have been popular for years and customers love them. A great add-on sale, OTABS

The Home Bait Shop – *Steps to Success*

have been in my shop since I started and have proven quite profitable. You can buy direct from the manufacturer at www.otabs.com Keeping your customers' bait alive in their buckets is just as important as keeping it alive in your own tank. OTABS work great and are inexpensive. There is great benefit to making sure the minnows you sell live up to customers' expectations, and OTABS helps you accomplish that. An added bonus is that it will add some extra profit to your sale!

If you are purchasing your Nightcrawlers and other worms in bulk, you will need a supply of cups to package the baits in retail-sized quantities. (**Purchasing your supply already packaged eliminates the need to buy empty containers and bedding separately...it also eliminates the counting.**) 8 ounce expanded polystyrene cups with vented lids work best for Nightcrawlers and Redworms.

Be sure to ask for 'squat' cups. Squat cups are low and wide, as opposed to tall, narrow cups used for drinks and the like. Taller, 'coffee-cup' type foam containers are top heavy and hard to stack. Use peat humus for bedding, or commercially prepared worm bedding such as **Buss Bed-Ding**. Buss Bed-Ding is cleaner than peat, which can be important for people with expensive boats. Many times people are reluctant to risk having messy peat humus turn to mud in their clean boat. The manufacturer's web site for Buss Bed-Ding has the

The Home Bait Shop – *Steps to Success*

full details about the product: www.magicproducts.com Follow instructions on the package to prepare the Buss Bed-Ding for packing the worms.

For smaller baits such as Mealworms or Waxworms, 3.5 ounce hard plastic cups and lids are best. Often called "portion cups," they are low-cost and sturdy. Manufactured by Solo and Fabri-Kal, these cups are pocket-sized and easy to handle.

Cricket containers are similar to minnow buckets in their ability to generate profits. Challenge Plastic Products also manufactures plastic 'buckets' designed to hold multiple quantities of live crickets. Cheaper containers made of paper are also available direct from cricket producers such as Hatley's Cricket Ranch.

<u>Do</u> consider using a cash register. Inexpensive units that print receipts are often available for under $100 from office supply stores. Alternatively, keep your eyes open in the classifieds (or eBay auction site) for used cash registers at big discounts. A cash register keeps your change organized, and provides a receipt for bait purchases. Some states require that receipts be given for live bait purchases, as they consider live minnows to be a regulated product. An inexpensive cash register can save you from writing out receipts by hand.

Now you are equipped with the basics of inventory and product packaging for your home bait shop.

Let's move on to pricing your products for success.

The Home Bait Shop – *Steps to Success*

The Home Bait Shop – *Steps to Success*

PRICING

I'll give some basic outlines for prices; however, it is best if you do some research on your own. If you are into fishing, you probably already have knowledge of the going rates for different types of bait in your area. If not, get on the phone! Most bait dealers will quote their retail prices to telephone callers. If you can't get prices that way, it will be necessary to visit some area retailers to get a grip on the competition's prices. Don't feel it necessary to undercut your competition's prices on each item. On the other hand, keep prices within reason or you will find a shortage of customers!

> **Fair, evenhanded pricing will keep your business profitable and insure repeat customers.**

I know of a few retailers who started their business with artificially low prices with the intent on snagging a customer base from the competition. The problem is you will have to be profitable some time, and that means an increase in your prices. Better to pick a fair price and stick with it. What follows are some price guidelines. Don't take these as hard and fast rules as geography has much to do with how much to charge. In addition, seasonal variations in pricing can affect the numbers at retail. Your own research is crucial here.

The Home Bait Shop – *Steps to Success*

Here's a quick review of average retail bait prices in 2017:

> Nightcrawlers: $2.75 per dozen
>
> Redworms: $3.75 per cup of 24
>
> Giant Mealworms: $2.25 per cup of 24
>
> Waxworms: $1.75 per cup of 24
>
> Small Golden Shiners: $2.50 per dozen
>
> Medium Golden Shiners: $4.75 per dozen
>
> Large Golden Shiners: $6.50 per dozen
>
> Extra Large Golden Shiners: $9.00 per dozen
>
> Crayfish: $4.00 per dozen
>
> Leeches: $5.00 per dozen

Buckets and small tackle items such as hooks, sinkers, OTABS, minnow dip nets and the like should be priced 50 to 125% over your cost. There are many opportunities for sidelines such as reel repairs, boat rental and the like. I'll discuss these other directions for your business in a later chapter.

The Home Bait Shop – *Steps to Success*

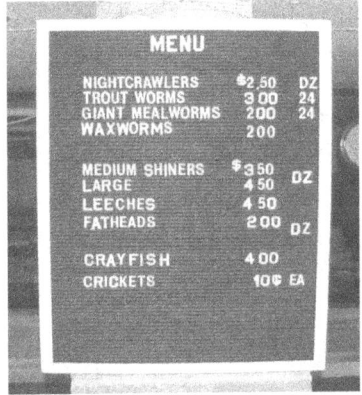

Keep your prices plainly marked in your shop. Because prices can sometimes change during the season, a letter board with changeable letters works great.

Now that you have a handle on common inventory items and an idea of pricing, let's work on advertising to get some feet through the door!

The Home Bait Shop – *Steps to Success*

ADVERTISING

There's an old saying that doing business without advertising is like winking in the dark. You know what you're doing, but no one else does. Some types of advertising are expensive. Some types are low cost but ineffective. I'll provide you with some ideas that have worked for me.

I've mentioned the importance of a good, lighted sign in a prior chapter. Your sign should be your starting point. Business cards are a good idea…but not right away. This is because business cards are usually given to people who already know about your business. If you can afford it, by all means have some printed. However, if funds are tight, this is something you can delay until you start making some money. I'll also provide you the contact for a terrific printer I've used for years.

You should, without fail, apply stickers with your business name and address to every bucket you sell.

This is essential. Stickers are a simple way to push the word-of-mouth concept along. Fishermen sharing a tale can easily see where the bait came from when your name is on the bucket. I've used bright yellow stickers with great success. Although almost gaudy, they certainly get noticed, and that's the whole point. The outdoor grade is best as water is certainly present on a bait bucket. Having your name on the bucket is particularly important with

The Home Bait Shop – *Steps to Success*

quality bait. Each healthy minnow in the bucket is advertising. Make sure people can easily see where the great minnows came from.

You may also wish to apply labels to cups of worms that you sell. However, labels are relatively expensive, and you may find that affixing a label to each worm container cuts into your profit to a large degree...not to mention the labor involved. Custom printed cups serve to lessen the cost per unit, although minimum quantities are somewhat high...50,000 or so.

Let's take a look at some 'conventional' advertising methods.

Local daily newspapers, unless featuring a special section on fishing, I've found to be a waste of money. Most newspapers are far too large and cluttered to have an effective ad with all but the largest budgets. Smaller "shopper" type newspapers are a better value but suffer from many of the same clutter problems as the dailies. Again, a special fishing section can be the exception. Do consider local newspaper web sites. Often the sites feature a fishing section, with updated information on fishing hot spots. This can be a great value and attaches your name to something relevant and timely.

Radio and television are mostly out of reach for this business. Local cable shows can be the exception, as well as cable advertising targeted to specific programs. Cable advertising has made great progress in recent years in its

The Home Bait Shop – *Steps to Success*

ability to target a specific demographic and geography. You can often find that your ideal audience can be reached with a budget that is entirely reasonable. It's worth looking into.

Often there are regional fishing and hunting publications that can be a great asset for your business. Advertising rates are generally reasonable, and these types of publications do get results. Check the Internet for listings of periodicals, or check for free publications at sporting goods stores and local tourist attractions in your area.

Do consider asking your customers how they heard of you. When running multiple advertising campaigns, it is useful to get a handle on what sources are working best for you. This allows you to spend your advertising dollars wisely, which is very important with a limited budget.

The most cost-effective advertising is word of mouth. This is the best form of advertising for the home bait shop. **Each referral amounts to a personal testimonial to the quality of your bait and service.**

It's important to be patient. Often it is hard to comprehend why customers are not beating down your door after you've spent so much time and effort getting your business up and running. Remember that people don't automatically know what you've done. You have to make sure they find out by using smart, effective, and economical methods to spread the word.

The Home Bait Shop – *Steps to Success*

The good news is that business brings business. Once you get the ball rolling, your base of customers will tell others, who tell others, and so on.

Don't forget about social media. Often free, it's easy to latch on to some built in traffic...perhaps even drawing visitors to your own web site.

Cultivation of an ever-increasing customer base will have an inverted-pyramid effect on the growth of your business...the more customers, the more referrals. The more referrals, the more customers. Great, right?

I promised you some information on sources for all that I have mentioned.

Next, we'll take a look at some suppliers I have used.

The Home Bait Shop – *Steps to Success*

WHOLESALERS AND SUPPLIERS

Here is a basic list of quality suppliers and contacts that I've found to be fair and straightforward.

Grayarc

P. O. Box 2944

Hartford, CT 06104-2944

(800) 243-5250   Fax (800) 292-4729

www.grayarc.com

Business Cards, printed labels, pens, and general business forms.

Jeff's Quality Baits

244 Bean Hill Road

Endicott, NY 13760

607-725-9364

Crayfish, Stone Cats (Madtoms), Hellgrammites

The Home Bait Shop – *Steps to Success*

Jumbo® Bait Company, Inc.

General Delivery 4

Hamilton, Ontario, Canada L8E 0G2

(800) 227-2248

www.jumbobait.com   www.jumbomealworms.com

Direct source for packaged Jumbo® Canadian Nightcrawlers, Dillies®, Duggers®, and Neons® shipped via UPS and FedEx worldwide.

I.F. Anderson Farms, Inc.

4377 Highway 70 West

Lonoke, AR 75208

(877) 467-2589

www.andersonminnows.com   www.blacksalty.com

Direct from the hatchery shipment of golden shiners and fatheads via FedEx. Also has a network of distributors nationwide.

The Home Bait Shop – *Steps to Success*

Triple S Sporting Supplies

325 Creekside Drive

Amherst, NY 14228

www.triplessportingsupplies.com

Terminal tackle wholesaler. Hooks, bobbers, rod/reel combos, fishing gear.

Seton Name Plate Company

PO Box 819

Branford, CT 06405

800-243-6624

www.seton.com

Custom made signage, stock retail signs, custom labels.

Jerry's Sport Center, Inc.

931 Dana Drive

Harrisburg, PA 17109

800-825-7060

The Home Bait Shop – *Steps to Success*

www.jerryssportscenter.com

Terminal tackle wholesaler. Hooks, bobbers, rod/reel combos, fishing gear. Shipping offered.

Rainbow Mealworms

PO BOX 4907

Compton, CA 90220

(310) 635-1494

www.rainbowmealworms.net

Mealworms in all sizes, as well as packing supplies.

Sure-Life Laboratories Corporation

PO Box 590

Seguin, TX 78156

830-372-2239

www.sure-life.com

Fish-keeping chemicals and related products.

The Home Bait Shop – *Steps to Success*

PROFITABLE SIDELINES

Your new bait shop will lend itself to an array of complementary services that can serve to increase your profitability and even out the annual revenue flow.

Rod and reel repair, or even custom rod building, offer the opportunity to keep you busy in the off-season. As most fishermen tend to put off repairs during the height of the season, the slower months of November thru February can be used to repair damaged gear. If you do your own repairs, this may be right up your alley. Most anglers are willing to pay for rod and reel maintenance service, so it is most certainly an avenue you should explore.

There are many distributors of rod blanks and rod building parts, as well as wholesalers of parts for major reel manufacturers. Don't hesitate to contact the manufacturers directly if you can't find a wholesaler. A trade publication such as *Fishing Tackle Retailer* can offer a wealth of information with regard to suppliers.

Boat and canoe rental also makes a great sideline. By purchasing low cost aluminum Jon boats and/or canoes, you can open up an avenue for extra sales.

Rental rates vary by area, so some research for your region is in order. A cash security deposit roughly matching the cost of the boat will be necessary for a successful rental operation. Some dealers accept credit

The Home Bait Shop – *Steps to Success*

cards, and this makes an attractive alternative to holding a cash deposit. Your local bank can provide details on accepting credit cards, which can benefit your main business as well.

It is important to provide personal flotation devices in a number matching the capacity of the boat or canoe. Oars should also be provided; perhaps with an extra-cost upgrade for an electric or gasoline motor to propel the craft.

Insurance for this endeavor is a must. Your local insurance agent can give you some idea of the costs involved.

Similar to renting boats, why not rent your own expertise? Offering a guide service can make an attractive sideline. If you are located in an area with high tourism, and are familiar with local fishing areas, a guide service would be a valuable addition to your shop. The added benefit, of course, is that you get to do more fishing yourself! Guide service rates vary, with day or half-day rates being the norm. This also can serve to spread the word about your bait shop if you promote your guide service with local hotels and resorts. I know many successful bait shop owners who have a part-time guide service on the side. Usually, the guide will provide bait, boat (along with the all-important flotation devices), gear, and expertise.

Repair work on outboard motors (electric and gasoline) can also make a nice sideline. It is worth noting that a

The Home Bait Shop – *Steps to Success*

factory-certified repair shop is usually required to do warranty work on motors. Factory certification for motor repair, although not impossible to obtain, almost certainly involves extra costs. If factory-certification interests you, contact the manufacturers. They will usually provide information on the procedure for certification.

Of course, there are obvious additions to your bait shop that require no real special preparation or arrangements. Hooks, bobbers, line, sinkers, and perhaps an informed selection of lures can make your shop more complete, **and more profitable**. Depending upon your area, dry flies may also be in demand. You can easily hook up with a local fly expert and offer his or her creations on consignment. This is another step to make your shop unique and profitable. The more reasons people have for coming into your shop, the more traffic that will be

The Home Bait Shop – *Steps to Success*

generated. Bodies in the store equal sales, so keep the interest in your shop as high as possible.

IMPORTANT NOTE: Although it is difficult to compete with the discount stores on price, it is worthwhile to remember that when buying bait, your customer is in **your** store. A complete selection of what the customer needs might just save that customer a trip to the discounters...and put the sale in your pocket. As a side note, it pays for you to visit the discounters every once and a while to keep tabs on the latest trends in fishing gear. A product you learn of through a discounter may look just as good on your wall of inventory.

Snacks, or perhaps a soda cooler, are also good ideas. Small, prepackaged selections of **gum and similar snacks** are a small investment that can pay fine dividends in profits. Search locally under "**Vending**" or "**Food Vendors.**" Consider Coke or Pepsi as well.

Some add-on items may not be directly related to bait, but have multiple purposes. Batteries are a good example. Anglers will need batteries for the small air pumps often used in bait buckets or live wells, and flashlights. All the best sporting goods wholesalers carry batteries, and you may find it profitable to add a selection to your inventory. (Not to mention being able to supply your own battery needs at wholesale prices!)

Surprisingly, I've found that rolls of low cost paper towels are great sellers. Something almost everyone forgets to grab from home, paper towels make cleaning fish, or just

The Home Bait Shop – *Steps to Success*

cleaning up the kids, a simple task. As with batteries, you also get the benefit of buying paper towels at bulk prices for your home use as well.

The more items you can put in the customer's hands, the better for you. If the angler is visiting your shop, there is no reason for him or her to leave without spending the maximum amount possible. There is nothing wrong with saving a customer a trip elsewhere, and there is also nothing wrong with having <u>your</u> shop get the sale. A good selection of add-on items is a key to achieve this goal, and will increase the amount of your average sales ticket.

The Home Bait Shop – *Steps to Success*

CONCLUSION

I hope this guide has provided you with some insight into what may become your new, successful business. I've attempted to give you a basic outline of some steps to take to increase your chances of building a successful live bait retailing venture.

I cannot stress enough that there is no substitute for experience, and there will be many instances where the services of a professional (attorney, accountant, insurance agent, etc.) are necessary to advise you and your business. It would be impossible for a guide such as this to provide you with detailed direction for your individual circumstance on these subjects.

It is important to give your new business time to grow. My own bait shop is still gathering new customers...even after over forty years. One must remember that the word of mouth advertising that suits the bait business best takes time, plain and simple. Don't get discouraged if it appears to be taking longer than you anticipated, as you will be building something that can endure.

Thank you so much for spending some of your time with this guide. I hope you have found it helpful and informative. I wish you the best of luck on your Steps to Success, with The Home Bait Shop!

= Epilogue =

As I put the finishing touches on the updates for the final printing of The Home Bait Shop, *Steps to Success*, I wanted to end with a personal note.

In the fall of 2012, I sold my business to a new owner and said goodbye to a way of life I had come to love. After spending four decades in the bait industry, it was time to move on. My wife and I embarked to a warmer climate, and I have to admit it's good to have my time to myself.

Looking back to the beginning, I have to say that I had no idea how successful a person could become selling something as simple as fishing bait. I had no idea how many lifelong friends I would come to know. I had no idea how rewarding it would be to spread my knowledge to others contemplating the same path via this publication. And I had no idea what it would feel like to finally give it all up and move on.

It's bittersweet, to pull out a cliché to describe this change. But, I wouldn't trade the memories and experiences for anything. I have been truly blessed.

J.B.

2 Corinthians 5:17

The Home Bait Shop – *Steps to Success*

---NOTES---

The Home Bait Shop – *Steps to Success*

---NOTES---

www.ingramcontent.com/pod-product-compliance
Lightning Source LLC
Chambersburg PA
CBHW030052230526
45471CB00003B/1061